Issues That Matter

Issues That Matter

✦

America's Moral Battleground

by Rob Hood

Edited by Melissa Evans

iUniverse, Inc.

New York Lincoln Shanghai

Issues That Matter
America's Moral Battleground

iUniverse books may be ordered through booksellers or by contacting:

iUniverse
2021 Pine Lake Road, Suite 100
Lincoln, NE 68512
www.iuniverse.com
1-800-Authors (1-800-288-4677)

ALL SCRIPTURES ARE TAKEN FROM THE
NEW INTERNATIONAL VERSION
LIFE APPLICATION STUDY BIBLE
BY
TYNDALE HOUSE PUBLISHERS
AND
ZONDERVAN PUBLISHING HOUSE

ISBN-13: 978-0-595-35667-6 (pbk)
ISBN-13: 978-0-595-80144-2 (ebk)
ISBN-10: 0-595-35667-2 (pbk)
ISBN-10: 0-595-80144-7 (ebk)

Printed in the United States of America

Contents

This book is written in memory of

Linda Ruth Dorroh Hood,

my late mother who guided me and led me through my life according to the teachings of God's word.

Train up a child in the way he should go, and when he is old, he will not turn from it.

—*Proverbs 22:6*

A MESSAGE OF THANKS

I want to say a word of thanks to all who made this book possible. First of all, I recognize and thank God for allowing this book to be possible. I also want to thank my family who has taught me well about having faith in God through Jesus Christ, and I thank my church family as well. The time I have spent with my church through the years of Vacation Bible School when I was a child, Bible Drill from fourth grade to twelfth, Sunday School, and sermons by my pastor have shaped my character and my faith, as well as, educated my knowledge of God's will and purpose through His son Jesus. Thank you all for believing in me!

DISCLAIMER

The events and topics of this book discussed by the author does not reflect specific facts according to modern science and does not prove modern scientific theories, ideas, and research to be false. The ideas discussed by the author and backed with Biblical scripture references are purely personal religious belief based on the Holy Bible's teachings and should not be interpreted as anything otherwise. The beliefs in this book about creation, abortion, homosexuality, Jesus Christ, and the review of active organizations listed within the contents of this work is meant to encourage Christians to preserve their traditional and conservative beliefs according to the word of God and the teachings of the Holy Bible and is not in any way meant to be discriminatory toward any individual, group, company, political organization, political party or religious belief or denomination. By the listed individuals and/or organizations within the contents of this publication, the author does not and will not endorse any specific political party or individual nor religious belief system or denomination.

Forethoughts: The Reason for the Writing

When I was just an early teenager, I dreamed of someday being a writer. I would write these wonderful and daring stories of far away worlds and heroes that could only come from the mind of a thirteen year old. I would pass my stories on to my friends who would read them and occasionally be persuaded to write something of their own. My eighth grade teacher told me after reading some of my stories that I should take the creative writing class when I enter tenth grade, but I never did. I always knew that I wanted to write a book but never knew exactly what I would write about, but I always assumed that it would be a science fiction or fantasy novel of some type because at the time I was utterly fascinated by otherworldly creatures, comic book heroes, and rock musicians which is usually the world of most typical teenage boys.

As I grew up, I eventually lost most of my interest in the science fiction world and began to take the world a little more seriously once I was in high school trying to pick a career path for myself. I made up my mind that I would go into the world of electronics; so after graduation I enrolled in Holmes Community College in Grenada, Mississippi, and after two years I received my Associate of Applied Science (AAS) degree in

Electronics Technology. However, during all the classes and term papers I had written through college, I never once stopped thinking about my book idea. I had been raised in a Christian home and taken to church almost every Sunday since I was a baby, but I not did begin to grow more in my faith until college even though I was saved years earlier. As my faith grew and I became more keenly aware of my worldly surroundings and what was happening to the Christian faith not only around the world, but also in my own country, I began to develop an interest in these events. I began to notice that modern politics and science was not at all friendly to the Christian faith in the United States. What I began to notice was that there were certain groups out there that wanted this message of hope in Jesus Christ gone from the public square. They wanted to totally change society to a pagan and worldly society with no mention of God. At last, I found my topic to write about.

In recent years alone I have witnessed a ridiculous barrage of attacks on Christianity by rogue groups making outlandish claims of freedom "from" religion. Abortion used to be the number one issue affecting America and the Christian faith. Certain left wing special interest groups who are supportive of abortion and so called "reproductive rights" usually make these silly attacks. I have even witnessed the unthinkable. One of these groups, and I won't call any of them by name because of legal purposes, had the bright idea of trying to get high school girls to be able to leave school or even be escorted from school to get an abortion of even birth control pills WITHOUT the consent of parents or even the knowledge of the parents. This same group wants to be able to distribute condoms at all schools and teach "safe sex" on school property. They want God gone but desire to teach our future generations to be even more immoral and corrupt adulterers than we are already used to seeing. (So much for reading, writing, and arithmetic.) It's really a shame and disgrace to see such a vulgar display of unrighteous behavior from an educated group of grown-up human beings, but on the Christian side of these things, there are counter attacks. There are numerous organizations out there fighting legal battles everyday for the cause of Godliness, repentance, return of moral values, and most of all, the return of good old-fashioned common sense. Some of these organizations are listed in the contents of this book.

Crisis pregnancy centers have popped up almost everywhere across America and have saved countless lives of unborn children. My own state of Mississippi has even cut abortions in half, but we still continue to fight for the lives and souls of the unborn victims of this hideous atrocity of secular America.

Abortion is now, I believe, the number two issue facing God's people across this great land and the free world today. Homosexuality has now taken center stage as the commanding issue all over the world. Homosexual activists, as well as abortion rights activists, constantly push for their personal agenda. They push for same sex marriage, civil rights as live-in couples, the right to terminate a pregnancy for any reason at all, and all of them relentlessly attack God's people with a continuous assembly line of lawyers devoted to demoralizing America.

There have been events here in America and internationally that have inspired my writing and conservative viewpoints even further. In January 2004 a priest was arrested in Sweden for speaking out about homosexuality, and the officials in Sweden claimed this was a hate crime and against international law. Since when has preaching the truth been against the law anywhere? Apparently Canada agrees with this so called international law because a preacher in Canada can now be imprisoned for preaching about homosexuality. It does get worse. The United States is having its own little version of persecution. On October 10, 2004, four Christians in Philadelphia, Pennsylvania were arrested and charged with numerous outlandish charges including four felonies for protesting at a gay pride event all while having a permit to do so, but charges were later dropped. I could have expected this type of behavior from a rogue terror-sponsored state or communist dictatorship but never from a free nation like America. If we don't act on these things now, our freedom to do so may not be present in the future. Things like this happen all the time, but our liberal-biased media simply refuse to report anything that might harm their political cause. Plainly speaking, they are afraid of the truth!

Atheist organizations, as well as groups like the American Civil Liberties Union (ACLU) and numerous others, have made consistent attacks on religion in America. We have tyrannical, out of control judges who strip us of our religious freedoms, liberties, and duties. Taking out the Ten Commandments is only the first step in a moral decline headed for a national disaster. Our very laws are based on these commandments that these judges rule unconstitutional. Congress has the power of impeachment for these controlling judges but fail to use that power because of political fear of not getting elected again. The people in this nation should take a stand and let our officials know that we want these judges removed from power.

Atheists have wanted for years to take the phrase "under God" out of our pledge of allegiance, and if they succeed at doing this, I, for one, will absolutely refuse to stand and pledge my allegiance to a nation without a God! Our first responsibility and allegiance is to God first and then our country because it was God who allowed this country to be formed in the first place. He made us and He can unmake us just as easily. All we need to do is continue on this path of immorality. It will anger God and he will destroy this nation just as he destroyed many other superior empires throughout the centuries that left Him for things of the world.

Christmas has been under attack for many years now, but no one is really standing up for this and I just cannot figure out why. Christmas parties at school are now being called "winter parties," and "Happy Holidays" is the national, politically correct replacement for Merry Christmas. It's not Christmas cards anymore; it's "Holiday Cards". Nativity scenes and even Christmas carols are being banned from the public now. As for me, and I hope you follow me in doing so, I will say Merry Christmas if I want to. and I will NOT buy from any retailer that posts "Happy Holidays" or "Seasons Greetings" in any store; nor will I honor any request for the removal of a carol or nativity scene. If these people cannot honor Jesus

Christ, the very reason for the whole celebration, then I don't need to honor them by giving them my money; and if schools say they want to ban a religious sounding song or carol or nativity scene from a Christmas play, then I would forbid my child from participating or maybe even attending that school at all.

While this is an age of computers and technology, I think we should call it the age of immorality and political correctness. We are witnessing an age in which it is wrong to confront militant Islamic terrorists who want freedom destroyed and replaced with militant style of Islam, but say it is okay to kill unborn children. Hard-line liberals across America blast the idea of war to preserve peace and freedom, and they cry out at losing less than 2,000 soldiers; but justify the brutal slaughter of over 42 million innocent unborn children. I do indeed hate to lose even one soldier and I hate war as much as anyone else, so don't call me unpatriotic. Call me supportive of the war effort unlike the biased media who NEVER report the good things happening, just the bad, again for their own political cause.

This is also an age where "God" is prohibited, but sin is rampant and repentance is slim to none. Bibles in schools have been banned and replaced with the teaching of "tolerance" of sinful behavior and lifestyles. The children of today face a much bigger problem than education reform. The very foundation of civilization and life itself has been taken and replaced with left wing liberal bias of politically correct tolerance of evolution, abortion, premarital sex, and homosexuality. Children are being diagnosed left and right with ADD and simply being given a pill to solve the problem. It seems like there is a pill for everything these days, but pills and tolerance will solve nothing. If we put back the institution of biblical right and wrong and Godly morality, let the teachers be teachers and have their authority for discipline back. Then 90 percent of the problem of facing violence and school problems will be solved. When children grow up believing there is no absolute right or wrong and have no discipline and no foundation to stand on, anything to believe in, or anyone to answer to, then that is a nation headed for disaster.

We as Christians have to start standing up for what is right before God judges and destroys this country that we fought so bravely to keep free. This book, though small in details, is aimed at stimulating enthusiasm and activism in the mind of the reader. I have purposefully left out specific facts and figures simply for the sake of having the reader to do the research for themselves by looking at the provided sources given at the end of this book or by other sources chosen by the reader. Anyone can write certain facts and figures on paper, but I feel it is better to point the reader in a certain direction of research to prove the truth to themselves and to the world. In the following pages, I now leave the decision to do so up to you!

The Battle Between Science and Religion

In this modern technologically advanced society that we live in and all of the scientific, technological, and medical breakthroughs we have to wonder in amazement at, there still remains a basic battle between science and Christianity. The well-known Charles Darwin is known around the world for his popular Theory of Evolution. This theory simply states that everything we see today evolved or changed from a relative or ancestor of its past. In other words, the theory explains how man slowly evolved over millions of years from apes. First of all, a theory is not fact. It is simply a proposal of a possible explanation of events during the course of a scientific study or observation.

There is a lot of objection to the theory of evolution within the Christian community. Let's take a look at what the Bible has to say about how the world came into existence.

In the Beginning God created the heavens and the earth. Now the earth was formless and empty, darkness was over the surface of the deep, and the Spirit of God was hovering over the waters. And God said, "Let there be light" and there was light. God saw that the light was good, and he separated the light from the darkness.

God called the light "day" and the darkness "night." And there was evening, and there was morning—the first day. And God said, "Let there be an expanse between the waters to separate water from water." So God made the expanse and separated the water under the expanse from the water above it. And it was so. God called the expanse "sky." And there was evening, and there was morning—the second day. And God said, "Let the water under the sky be gathered to one place and let dry ground appear." And it was so. God called the dry ground "land," and the gathered waters he called "seas." And God saw that it was good. Then God said "Let the land produce vegetation: seed-bearing plants and trees on the land that bear fruit with seed in it, according to their various kinds." And it was so. The land produced vegetation: plants bearing seed according to their kinds and trees bearing fruit with seed in it according to their kinds. And God saw that it was good. And there was evening and there was morning—the third day. And God said, "Let there be lights in the expanse of the sky to separate day from night, and let them serve as signs to mark seasons and days and years, and let them be lights in the expanse of the sky to give light on the earth." And it was so. God made two great lights—the greater light to govern the day and the lesser light to govern the night. He also made the stars. God set them in the expanse of the sky to give light on earth, to govern the day and the night, and to separate light from darkness. And God saw that it was good. And there was evening and there was morning—the fourth day. And God said, "Let the water teem with living creatures, and let the birds fly above the earth across the expanse of the sky." So God created the great creatures of the sea and every living and moving thing with which the water teems, according to their kinds, and every winged bird according to its kind. And God saw that it was good. God blessed them and said, "Be fruitful and increase in number and fill the water in the seas, and let the birds increase on earth." And there was evening, and there was morning—the fifth day. And God said, "Let the land produce living creatures according to their kinds: livestock, creatures that move along the ground, and wild animals, each according to its kind." And it was so. God made the wild animals according to their kinds, the livestock according to their kinds, and all the creatures that move along the ground according to their kinds. And God saw that it was good. Then God said, "Let us make man in our own image, in our likeness, and let them rule over the fish of the sea and the birds of the air, over the livestock, over all the earth, and over the creatures that move along the ground." So God created man in his own image, and in the image of God he created him; male and female he created them. God blessed them and said to them, "Be fruitful and increase in number; fill the earth and subdue it. Rule over the fish of the sea and the birds of the air and over every living creature that moves on the ground." Then God said, "I give you every seed-bearing plant on the face of the whole earth and every tree that has fruit with seed in it. They will be yours for food. And to all the beasts of the earth and all the birds of the air and all the creatures that move on the ground—everything that has the breath of life in it—I give every green plant for food." And it was so. God saw all he had made, and it was very good. And there evening and there was morning—the sixth day. Thus the heavens and the earth were completed in all their vast array. By the seventh day God had finished the work he had been doing; so on the seventh day he rested from all his work. And God *blessed the seventh day and made it holy, because on it he rested from all the work of creating he had done.*

—(Genesis 1–2:1-3)

I am completely convinced that when the Bible says "In the beginning God" that God literally created the universe and that these verses plainly state that God is who He says He is. He is the Alpha and Omega, the First and the Last, and above all else, the Creator of life, the universe and everything in it. Our modern scientists along with some educators fill our children's minds at school with the shameful event of saying that all matter in the universe was at one time existing in a ball of material and exploded to create our universe. They claim that our universe expanded and is still expanding. It starts there by defiling and belittling God to His own face. No wonder children are killing children in our school system. The public education system is a mess since God was thrown out, and the door locked behind Him. Let's face it. When children are not even told the truth about where they come from and about their very creation and existence, how can they respect life itself? They don't have a place or purpose in life. Knowing that you are created by an all-powerful God puts a new perspective on life and the universe itself. God keeps on knocking at the door of our public education system since He was expelled, but some educators and left wing radicals refuse to let Him in thinking He is a threat and not realizing that all He wants to do is help.

You saw how God created the universe and man, now let's take a look at the creation of woman and the purpose for all creation.

The Lord God said, "It is not good that man be alone. I will make a helper suitable for him." Now the Lord God had formed out of the ground all the beasts of the field and all the birds of the air. He brought them to the man to see what he would name them; and whatever the man called each living creature, that was its name. So the man gave names to all the livestock, the birds of the air and all the beasts of the field. But for Adam no suitable helper was found. So the Lord caused the man to fall into a deep sleep; and while he was sleeping, he took one of the man's ribs and closed up the place with flesh. Then the Lord God made a woman from the rib he had taken out of the man, and he brought her to the man. The man said, "This is now bone of my bones and flesh of my flesh; she shall be called woman for she was taken out of man." For this reason a man will leave his father and his mother and be united with his wife, and they will become one flesh.

—(Genesis 2:18-25)

While Jesus was talking one day to the Pharisees about marriage and divorce he made mention of the creation.

"But at the beginning of creation God made them male and female".

—(Mark 10:6)

By this I hope that you may see that creation is made by God and for God while evolution is a thought or an idea made by man and for man. The creation of the universe and all of its components right down to mankind was made to praise and glorify God. Man was created in the very image of God himself. He chose to give us the ability to reason, to be creative, to love, to communicate in the form of an organized speech we call language, and the ability to made complicated decisions. No other animal was created with the intelligence and abilities that man was given which was intended to be for the sole purpose of communication with the Creator.

If you take a look at nature, you can surely see God's paintbrush of creation all over. Take a look into the night sky. The stars are too many to be counted. We see uncountable galaxies from photos our telescopes have taken. We are amazed at the beauty of the mountains and at the nature of wildlife. The Earth spins exactly the same now as it did when it was created. The human body itself is amazing. Doctors and scientists still have not learned everything about the human body even with our modern technology. Each cell and each organ has its own specific function and duty to perform. Seemingly simple things in nature are still a mystery to mankind such as how bees make honey. There are so many countless little things in life that are stunning yet could not happen by chance as our scientists would have you to believe. Do you think that everything you see every day throughout this world and the whole universe was just an accident or happened by chance? No way! God had a hand in it. There can simply be no other explanation. I am convinced that I am not related to an ape such as our biology text books will teach our children. My former pastor made a serious but rather comical statement one Sunday morning about man evolving from apes and how we have become so wicked in our culture that if we did evolve from them, then maybe we need to apologize to the apes for our behavior. It's funny, but true. The very idea of man evolving from apes or anything else is a slap in the face of God and any follower to Jesus Christ. If these people with the evolution idea want to claim kin to an ape, that's fine by me, but I was created by a Holy, magnificent, righteous, pure, and loving God who made me for the purpose of serving Him. King David seemed to have the same idea about being made to serve God just like I do. King David believed that only fool-hearted people do not believe in God.

The fool says in his heart,
"There is no God."
They are corrupt, their deeds are vile;
there is no one who does good.

The Lord looks down from Heaven
on the sons of men
to see if there are any who understand,
any who seek God.

All have turned aside,
they have together become corrupt;

there is no one who does good,
not even one.

Will evildoers never learn-
those who devour my people as men eat bread
and who do not call on the Lord?
There they are, overwhelmed with dread,
for God is present in the company of the righteous.
You evildoers frustrate the plans of the poor,
but the Lord is their refuge.

—(Psalms 14: 1-6)

I cannot really imagine what it is like to not have a permanent belief system in something. Believing that God created the universe is comforting to know but I just cannot grasp the idea of this whole universe existing accidentally. I am completely convinced that there is a just and loving God who is the creator of all life and the whole universe and we must continue to stress this to our children who are being bombarded by an anti-God counter culture in our education system. It is important that they know the truth about the origins of life so that our future generations will have the reverence, respect, and morality for life and the desire to serve the Creator who wants our attention and our love for Him more than anything.

Choose Life or Choose Death

In recent years the battle over abortion has really heated up on both sides of the issue. On the pro-abortion side, they believe that a woman has the sole right of reproduction referred to as the "right to choose." On the pro-life side, they believe that life begins at conception and abortion under any circumstance is murder. I for one stand with the pro-life stance believing abortion is a crime. I believe, as many do, that at conception, there is a soul given to that growing being inside the mother's womb and that taking the life of this tiny human in the womb is disrupting God's plan for that child.

The pro-choice people try to justify their cause by changing the circumstances altogether. For example, they will give their classic argument of "Well, what if a woman is raped and becomes pregnant?" That indeed is a sad and unfortunate situation to be in, but still does not justify murdering the innocent, unborn child. In this case that is heavily pressed by pro-abortionists and radical leftists, only the situation has changed, not the issue. God still has a plan for this unborn human no matter what circumstances it was conceived under. I can understand that woman who may result in pregnancy due to rape will not really want that child, but there are alternatives to abortion. Killing that child should not be an option. It has every right to live as freely as we do. We must not let pro-choice activists change our stance on this issue by implementing circumstances that has very little chance of happening to start with. This is simply a ploy to continue their campaign of selfish ambitions to choose death over life for their own interests. In other words, they don't like responsibility. The majority of abortion activists simply refuse to take on the responsibility of a child. Teens have sex before marriage, which is wrong and unbiblical itself, then the girl gets pregnant and faces enormous pressure by her so-called friends to have an abortion so that she may have a chance to go to college, have a career, or have a "life." In this case abortion, would be the easy way out of an irresponsible and totally preventable situation. Instead of taking responsibility for their actions, they may choose to take a life to create a better situation for themselves.

The psalmist David described being knit together or made by God and of being of great importance to God even before he was born.

For you created my inmost being;
you knit me together in my mother's womb.
I praise you because I am fearfully and wonderfully made;
your works are wonderful,
I know that full well.
My frame was not hidden from you in that secret place.
When I was woven together in the depths of the earth,

> *your eyes saw my unformed body.*
> *All the days ordained for me*
> *were written in your book*
> *before one of them came to be.*

> —(Psalm 139: 13-16)

Not only did David mention being important to God while in the womb, but God himself told the prophet Jeremiah that he was formed in the womb for a purpose to serve Him.

> *The word of the Lord came to me, saying,*
> *"Before I formed you in the womb I knew you,*
> *Before you were born I set you apart;*
> *I appointed you as a prophet to the nations.*

> —(Jeremiah 1: 4-5)

God still does the same thing today. He creates each and every one of us in His own image and forms us in the womb to serve Him. This is the primary argument concerning abortion. The pro-choice advocates simply do not see this issue as Christians see it. They do not understand that God has a plan and a will for that unborn child that is murdered for selfish gains. I believe that on judgment day when we all stand before Jesus Christ on His throne, these people will have to give an account for their actions.

I feel that at a certain stage in the womb, these infants feel certain emotions and pain. Look at what happened to John the Baptist while in his mother's womb.

At that time Mary got ready and hurried to a town in the hill country of Judea, where she entered Zechariah's home and greeted Elizabeth. When Elizabeth heard Mary's greeting, the baby leaped in her womb, and Elizabeth was filled with the Holy Spirit. In a loud voice she exclaimed: "Blessed are you among women, and blessed is the child you will bear!"

—(Luke 1:39-42)

This infant who was John the Baptist instantly recognized Jesus for who he was even before they were born. These unborn children do have, I believe, feelings of pain at a later stage of development and taking this life at any stage is murder. You hear all the time the pro-choice supporters yelling, "We have a right to choose," and they do choose. They choose death instead of life. They murder a life that God has a plan for and that Jesus came and died to save.

Christians do agree with the biblical teachings about the age of accountability. This is simply the age at which a person can be held accountable before God for his or her actions. This is not a definite age since individuals mature at different levels. However, we as grown-up human beings will be held accountable for our actions whether good or bad, whether we choose life or choose death. I believe that the day when abortions become illegal and Roe v. Wade is overturned, there will be a party both for Christians here on earth and for the angels in heaven who will be rejoicing while God smiles with joy and satisfaction for a decision made by His creation, man, to once again follow Him and not the wiles of the devil.

Diversified Sin: The Church versus the World

A man is forewarned by two strangers with whom her has grown to trust that a powerful disaster is coming soon. Therefore, he gathers his wife and two daughters, and they all run frantically out of the house and head for another town miles away to escape certain doom. As the sun rises, it casts a shadow over what used to be a thriving city that is now in ruins. The city and all forms of life including humans, animals, and all vegetation is lying in ashes destroyed by fire from the sky. The family that escaped was safe until the wife turns to see her destroyed but beloved home, and as she turns to look back at her city, she is instantly consumed and turned into a pillar of salt.

This sounds like a modern sci-fi action thriller but its not. This is the true story of God destroying a wicked city riddled with homosexual lifestyles as a normal way of living. You can read it for yourself:

The two angels arrived at Sodom in the evening, and Lot was sitting in the gateway of the city. When he saw them, he got up to meet them and bowed with his face to the ground. "My Lords," he said, "please turn aside to your servant's house. You can wash your feet and spend the night and then go on your way early in the morning." "No," they answered, "we will spend the night in the square." But he insisted so strongly that they did go with him and entered his house. He prepared a meal for them, baking bread without yeast, and they ate. Before they had gone to bed, all the men from every part of the city of Sodom—both young and old—surrounded the house. They called to Lot, "Where are the men who came to you tonight? Bring them out to us so that we can have sex with them." Lot went outside to meet them and shut the door behind him and said, "No, my friends. Don't do this wicked thing. Look, I have two daughters who have never slept with a man. Let me bring them out to you, and you can do what you like with them. But don't do anything to these men, for they have come under protection of my roof." "Get out of our way," they replied. And they said "This fellow came here as an alien, and now wants to play judge! We'll treat you worse than them." They kept bringing pressure on Lot and moved forward to break down the door. But the men inside reached out and pulled Lot back into the house and shut the door. Then they struck the men who were at the door of the house, young and old, with blindness so that they could not find the door. The two men said to Lot, "Do you have anyone else here—sons-in-law, sons or daughters, or anyone else in the city who belongs to you?

Get them out of here, because we are going to destroy this place. The outcry of the Lord against its people is so great that he has sent us to destroy it." So Lot went out and spoke to his sons-in-law, who were pledged to marry his daughters. He said, "Hurry and get out of this place, because the Lord is about to destroy the city!"

But his sons-in-law thought he was joking. With the coming of dawn, the angels urged Lot, saying, "Hurry! Take your wife and your two daughters who are here, or you will be swept away when the city is punished." When he hesitated, the two men grasped his hand and the hands of his and of his two daughters and led them safely out of the city, for the Lord was merciful to them. As soon as they had brought them out, one of them said, "Flee for your lives! Don't look back, and don't stop anywhere in the plain! Flee to the mountains or you will be swept away!" But Lot said to them, "No my lords, please! Your servant has found favor in your eyes, and you have shown great kindness to me in sparing my life. Look, here is a town near enough to run to, and it is small. Let me flee to it—it is very small isn't it? Then my life will be spared." He said to him, "Very well, I will grant this request too; I will not over-throw the town you speak of. But flee there quickly, because I can-not do anything until you reach it." (That is why the town is called Zoar.) By the time Lot reached Zoar, the sun had risen over the land. Then the Lord rained down burning sulfur on Sodom and Gomorrah—from the Lord out of the heavens. Thus he over-threw those cities and the entire plain, including all those living in the cities—and also the vegetation in the land. But Lot's wife looked back, and she became a pillar of salt. Early the next morn-ing Abraham got up and returned to the place where he had stood before the Lord. He looked down toward Sodom and Gomorrah, toward all the plain land, and he saw dense smoke rising from the land, like smoke from a furnace. So when God destroyed the cities of the plain, he remembered Abraham, and he brought Lot out of the catastrophe that overthrew the cities where Lot had lived.

—(Genesis 19:1-29)

We see by this story that God destroyed these two cities because they had grown so wicked with rampant homosexuality and incest, but homosexuality has been going on since the beginning of civilization. It's nothing new, but in this secular world in which we live there are those today and in our own great nation of America that are determined to undermine God's plan of marriage between one man and one woman by saying it's "equal rights" or even "civil rights" to marry same-sex couples. They have hijacked the name of civil rights for their own goals.

The radical leftists label this behavior as "tolerance" and "diversity", but there is a distinct difference between diversity and sin. Homosexuality is a sin before God no matter what others might say. These same left-wing extremists have the audacity to try to infiltrate the minds of children at schools across America by teaching "tolerance" of these sinful life-styles. They have taken away prayer, the Bible, the acknowledgement of God and Jesus, and exchanged righteous teachings of moral and ethical responsibility for sinful fantasies and in doing so have corrupted our future generations.

The Bible, God's holy, righteous, and infallible word, speaks very clearly about this behavior and how God views this type of lifestyle.

Do not lie with a man as one lies with a woman; that is detestable.

—(Leviticus 18:22)

If a man lies with a man as one lies with a woman, both of them have done what is detestable. They must be put to death; their blood is on their heads.

—(Leviticus 20:13)

I don't personally agree that the death penalty is the correct way of dealing with this issue. I included this verse to show the mentality God has for this type behavior. These are the words he told Moses. Homosexuality is sickening to society and to God and it corrupts our culture with disease and demoralizes the population of America.

Paul stated in his writing to the Romans about God's anger and wrath toward this sinful lifestyle and how He will judge those guilty of it.

Therefore God gave them over in the sinful desires of their hearts to sexual impurity for the degrading of their bodies with one another. They exchanged the truth of God for a lie, and worshipped and served created things rather than the Creator—who is forever praised. Amen. Because of this, God gave them over to shameful lusts. Even their women exchanged natural relations for unnatural ones. In the same way the men also abandoned natural relations with women and were inflamed with lust for one another. Men committed indecent acts with other men, and received in themselves the due penalty for their perversion. Furthermore, since they did not think it worthwhile to retain the knowledge of God, he gave them over to a depraved mind, to do what ought not to be done. They have become filled with every kind of wickedness, evil, greed and depravity. They are full of

*envy, murder, strife, deceit, and malice. They are gossips, slander-
ers, God-haters, insolent, arrogant and boastful; they invent ways
of doing evil; they disobey their parents; they are senseless, faithless,
heartless, ruthless. Although they know God's righteous decree that
those who do such things deserve death, they not only continue to
do these very things but also approve of those who practice them.
You, therefore, have no excuse, you who pass judgment on someone else, for at whatever point you judge the other, you are con-
demning yourself, because you who pass judgment do the same
things. Now we know that God's judgment against those who do
such things is based on the truth. So when you, a mere man, pass
judgment on them and yet do the same things, do you think you
will escape God's judgment? Or do you show contempt for the
riches of his kindness, tolerance, and patience, not realizing that
God's kindness leads to repentance? But because of your stubborn-
ness and your unrepentant heart, you are storing up wrath against
yourself for the day of God's wrath, when his righteous judgment
will be revealed. God "will give to each person according to what
he has done." To those who by persistence in doing good seek glory,
honor and immortality, he will give eternal life. But for those who
are self-seeking and who reject the truth and follow evil, there will
be wrath and anger. There will be trouble and distress for every
human being who does evil: first for the Jew, then for the Gentile;
but glory, honor and peace for everyone who does good: first for the
Jew, then for the Gentile. For God does not show favoritism.*

—(Romans 1: 24-31, 2: 1-11)

As we read these scripture we see how God reacts to this
type of behavior. Marriage and the union of the family was

supposed to be devotion to God between one man and one woman. That's the way that God created it and intended it to be. Things changed after the incident in the Garden of Eden and sin entered the world and society became evil and corrupt and did not even want to worship the Lord God nor obey His laws. Today around the word, the sanctity of marriage and its role in society is under constant attack by those who prefer "tolerance and diversity" before Godliness and righteousness. We must protect marriage and the family by activist judges and rogue extremists who defy God and His creation by defiling his Holy laws. The only hope to solve this problem that we face as a civil society is to proclaim the message of Jesus Christ. He died for everyone no matter what they have done or who they are. We have to act now before America becomes another Sodom and Gomorrah and is destroyed completely by the very God who allowed it to be founded. If America continues on this path of "tolerant and diverse" lifestyle choices like these, we can be sure of God's wrath and judgment against our own nation, but all that can change if we repent, trust in Jesus, and turn back to God as a country, just as God's own people of Israel have done so many times before.

The Case for the Commandments

In recent years extreme left wing individuals and organizations have constantly attacked the Ten Commandments' displays and have vowed to remove them from the eye of the public. They all agree on two statements that they take from the Constitution. The first argument deals with Amendment I of the United States Constitution which simply states that congress cannot establish religion. Congress has never and is not now establishing religion. When something is established, it is permanent. Our forefathers created this part of the amendment in order that one particular religion would not be recognized as the national religion because this would restrict religious freedom. For example, the government cannot establish Christianity, Islam, or any other religion or religious belief or denomination as the official national religious system whereby all must follow or adhere to. Establishment of religion and recognition and respect of religion are two different meanings. Our leaders seek to legislate according to the majority of the people's personal religious belief system, not establish a system which everyone has to follow. This is a misleading argument lead by America's top anti-God organizations who wish to take away all symbols of Christianity from the public. They abuse the system by declaring false assumptions and mislead-ing the public about what is constitutional and what is not.

The second argument comes from the whole separation of church and state sentence. This statement is not even in the Constitution. It actually originated from a letter written by Thomas Jefferson to a group of Baptists in Danbury, Con-necticut that stated simply that a national religion could not be established by the government. Jefferson never intended for religious beliefs not to have an effect on government's public policies as the liberal mainstream culture has us to believe. This argument of separation of church and state does not mean that religion is banned from state and federal policy; it only means that government cannot back a religious belief and force this belief on the public. Don't let the liberal leftists con-vince you otherwise. This argument is just another ploy to take God out of the public square.

The Ten Commandments are in many public places and are being challenged to be taken down because of these false arguments being made in the court system and lawsuits made by organizations that think that we don't need God. I com-mend Judge Roy Moore for his decision to yield to a higher authority (God) and not to give in to a court order to remove the Ten Commandments monument from his Montgomery, Alabama courthouse. He is a man of God and has shown that he has integrity and honor. He recognizes that it was God who is responsible for his very existence and for position as Chief Justice. We need more men like him on the benches as Chief Justice who are willing to stand up to the world for what is right.

The Ten Commandments that Judge Moore stood up for and that Christians are fighting to keep the right of have been around for a long time. These laws were given to Moses by God after he led the Israelites out of Egypt and although these laws are centuries old and were originally given to God's chosen people, we too are subject to these laws even today. I won't go into great detail about the whole story of the relationship between Egypt and the Jews and how Moses led them out of Egypt to the promised land because it is a lengthy story and actually begins with Abraham in Genesis. You can read it for yourself from Genesis 11—Exodus 20. These scriptures will give ample history from the time after the flood of Noah until the Ten Commandments were given. Let's look at what happened as the commandments were given.

And God spoke these words:

"I am the Lord your God, who brought you out of Egypt, out of the land of slavery. You shall have no other Gods before me. You shall not make for yourself an idol in the form of anything in heaven above or on the earth beneath or in the waters below. You shall not bow down to them or worship them; for I, the Lord your God, am a jealous God, punishing the children for the sin of the fathers to the third and fourth generation of those who hate me, but showing love to a thousand generations of those who love me and keep my commandments. You shall not misuse the name of the Lord your God, for the Lord will not hold anyone guiltless who misuses his name. Remember the Sabbath day by keeping it holy. Six days you shall labor and do all your work, but the sev-

enth day is a Sabbath to the Lord your God. On it you shall not do any work, neither your son or daughter, nor your manservant or maidservant, nor your animals, nor the alien within your gates. For in six days the Lord made the heavens and the earth, the sea, and all that is in them, but he rested on the seventh day. Therefore the Lord blessed the Sabbath day and made it holy. Honor your father and mother, so that you may live long in the land the Lord your God is giving you. You shall not murder. You shall not commit adultery. You shall not steal. You shall not give false testimony against your neighbor. You shall not covet your neighbor's house. You shall not covet your neighbor's wife, or his manservant or maidservant, his ox or donkey, or anything that belongs to your neighbor."

When the people saw the thunder and lightening and heard the trumpet and saw the mountain in smoke, they trembled in fear. They stayed at a distance and said to Moses, "Speak to us yourself and we will listen. But do not have God speak to us or we will die." Moses said to the people, "Do not be afraid. God has come to test you, so that the fear of God will be with you to keep you from sinning." The people remained at a distance, while Moses approached the thick darkness where God was.

—(Exodus 20: 1-21)

These commandments still apply to our society today, and our country's very foundation of law was based upon the commandments of God. Many radical liberals no longer want these commandments to remain in the public square. Think about this. Every crime committed anywhere in the world breaks one of these commandments. If you kill someone, that falls under "You shall not murder." The identity theft and all other manner of theft that plagues our society today would fall under "You shall not steal." If you lie to someone or lie under oath, that would fall under "You shall not give false testimony against your neighbor." The list goes on and on.

I firmly believe that the Ten Commandments played a vital role in the founding of our country and our laws since our forefathers were Christians and prayed daily to God for guidance as to how to base and establish our system of government. If our forefathers who founded this nation on the belief in God and His creation of all existence could somehow see how our Constitution is being rewritten by radical leftists judges who are unelected and unaccountable, they would probably roll over in their graves.

The whole argument of separation of church and state is rather ironic. Government is allowed and even ordained by God. It is God who allowed a system of organized leadership as government to even take place to start with.

Everyone must submit himself to the governing authorities, for there is no authority except that which God has established. The authorities that exist have been established by God.

—(Romans 13:1)

God allowed mankind to form a legal system of accountability so that we could have a system of justice in our society. While our government cannot establish religion, the people who elect our officials and the officials who are elected still have the right to recognize and worship God as they please according to the first amendment of our Constitution that allows us to do so. It is only when our leaders force a particular religious belief or practice onto the people and command that they obey this that actual establishment occurs. This has never happened and is not happening now. We must continue to pray for and elect Godly leaders who recognize the idea of true freedom as our founding fathers did. We must continue to follow the path of truth and freedom through a real democracy that recognizes God as the very reason for our existence.

The Name that Changes Everything

All around the world sin is rampant. Just in the United States alone we see all types of sinful and unjust activities every day. We witness everything from murder, robbery, substance abuse, cheating, lying, adultery, and the list goes on. The subjects that you have read about in this book and the activities just mentioned have a distinct name and that name is sin. There is also another name, but this name is the opposite from sin. As a matter of fact, this name changes the whole picture by removing sin. That name is Jesus Christ and the consequences of following Him is everlasting life.

Jesus, we are told in the scriptures, is the son of God who was born of a virgin and came here willingly to die for our sins in our place so that anyone who would believe in Him would have eternal life through him. He did not have to come here and die. He chose to because it was the will of the Father.

Jesus performed many miracles while here on earth which included making the blind to see, the deaf to hear, and the lame to walk, calming storms, casting out demons, walking on water, and raising the dead. While he amazed all who followed him with miracles and parables, his ultimate purpose was to die for our sins.

For the Son of Man came to seek and to save what was lost.

—(Luke 19:10)

Even today, as in previous history, people continue to believe that there is more than one way to get to heaven. Other religions have their own ideas about how to get into the kingdom of heaven and how they will live in the afterlife. The most common myth about going to heaven is by believing that being good and not doing anything wrong, reading the Bible, going to church, and helping others, will get them into God's kingdom, but that is not true. While all of these things are good to do and important, doing these things alone and not being saved and having a relationship with Jesus Christ will result in dying and going to hell just like all others who are not saved. Salvation is the key to the gates of God's holy city. The Bible simply teaches that Jesus is the only way to have eternal life in heaven.

"I am the resurrection and the life. He who believes in me will live, even though he dies; and whoever lives and believes in me will never die. Do you believe this?"

—(John 11:25)

Salvation is found in no one else, for there is no other name under heaven given to men by which he must be saved.

—(Acts 4:12)

Jesus answered, "I am the way and the truth and the life. No one comes to the father except through me."

—(John 14:6)

Remember that Jesus said He was **THE** way. Not one way or some way or a way, but **THE** way. In other words, it's just like the verse reads. Jesus is the only ticket to heaven.

Let's look at our only two choices in the afterlife. Now, whether you like it or not you are going to spend eternity somewhere, and it's up to you where you are going to spend it. It will either be in heaven with Jesus or in hell with the devil and his angels. Let's compare the two. Heaven will be wonderful. It will be a place completely free from sin, sickness, and death.

The angel who talked with me had a measuring rod of gold to measure the city, its gates and its walls. The city was laid out like a square, as long as it was wide. He measured the city with the rod and found it to be 12,000 stadia (1,400 miles) in length, and as wide as was long. He measured its walls and it was 144 cubits (200 feet) thick by man's measurement, which the angel was using. The wall was made of jasper, and the city of pure gold, as pure as glass. The foundations of the city walls were decorated with every kind of precious stone. The first foundation was jasper, the second sapphire, the third chalcedony, the fourth emerald, the fifth sardonyx, the sixth carnelian, the seventh chrysolite, the eighth beryl, the ninth topaz, the tenth chrysoprase, the eleventh jacinth, and the twelfth amethyst. The twelve gates were twelve pearls, each made of a single pearl. The great street of the city was of pure gold, like transparent glass. I did not see a temple in the city, because the Lord God Almighty and the Lamb are its temple. The city does not need the sun or the moon to shine on it, for the glory of God gives it light, and the Lamb is its lamp. The nations will walk by its light, and the kings of the earth will bring their splendor into it. On no day will its gates ever be shut, for there will be no night there. The glory and honor of the nations will be brought into it. Nothing impure will ever enter it, nor will any-one who does what is shameful or deceitful, but only those whose names are written in the Lamb's book of life.

—(Revelation 21: 15-27)

He will wipe every tear from their eyes. There will be no more death or mourning or crying or pain, for the old order of things has passed way.

—(Revelation 21:4)

Wow! Heaven! What a great place to live. I cannot imagine living for eternity in a place with no sin, sickness, or death. Hell, on the other hand, is much different. Hell is described in the New Testament as a place of eternal fire and torment. A place of weeping and gnashing of teeth. Jesus came and died and then rose again so that all who would believe in Him would have eternal life with Him in heaven. Hell was origi-nally meant for Satan and his angels. It was not meant for man. When Jesus returns, and he will, all who have ever lived and is living now will be judged. All whose names are not recorded in the Book of Life will be cast into hell for eternity.

Then I saw a great white throne and him who was seated on it. Earth and sky fled from his presence, and there was no place for them. And I saw the dead, great and small standing before the throne, and the books were opened. Another book was opened, which was the book of life. The dead were judged according to what they had done as recorded in the books. The sea gave up its dead that were in it, and death and Hades gave up the dead that were in them, and each person was judged according to what he had done. Then death and Hades were thrown into the lake of fire. The lake of fire is the second death. If anyone's name was not found written in the book of life, he was thrown into the lake of fire.

—(Revelation 20:11-15)

Many unsaved or unbelievers ask the same question about God. "If God is so loving and caring why does he send you to hell?" The fact of the matter is that God has never sent anyone to hell. God loves you and wants to accept you into His kingdom but He cannot allow sin to enter into heaven, so you have to be cleansed of your sin and appear unto God as pure and undefiled. Your name has to be written in the lamb's book of life. The way to do that is to accept Jesus as your savior and he will wash your sins away and you will be able to enter heaven when the time comes. It's when a person willingly rejects this magnificent plan through Jesus that he sends himself to hell. He was calling you, and it was you that rejected Him and in the judgment He will reject you. When your name is not called for being in the book of life, he will cast you into hell.

Once in hell, there will be no turning back. You will be there for eternity. You will wish for death, but death will not come. Death was defeated and destroyed when Christ died and rose again. Men rejected Jesus and judged him. He was mocked, beaten, spat upon, cursed, and then crucified, and He did it all willingly for everyone who would believe on Him. When He was on the cross, He could have called for ten thousand angels and they would have immediately taken Him off of that cross and carried Him back to heaven, but He did not do this. He chose to die willingly for you.

You can have eternal life and a guarantee that your name is in the book of life never to be erased if you repent, ask for forgiveness, and give your life to Him. No sin is unforgivable. You past does not matter. All of that can be swept clean and made new if you will just ask and then receive. You need first to realize that you are a sinner and need to change your ways or repent and ask for forgiveness and put your faith in Jesus Christ by expressing your desire to follow Him. You can receive Jesus through prayer. It could be a simple prayer similar to this:

Dear Heavenly Father, I know that I am a sinner and have displeased you in many ways, and I want to change. I do believe that you died to save me from my sins and were resurrected from death so that I might have eternal life. Will you please forgive me for my sins? I want to turn from my sins and ask you to come into my life and my heart as my personal lord and savior. From now on I will live a life pleasing to you. Thank you for your grace, love, and forgiveness. Amen!

Now that you know how to be saved and your name recorded forever in the book of life, you will have no excuse on judgment day when Jesus asks you about your life. There will be a day of judgment when all will have to give an account of every word, thought, and action whether good or bad. The first time Jesus came, he came as a baby wrapped in swaddling clothes lying in a manger. The next time he comes, he will come as King of Kings and Lord of Lords where every knee will bow and every tongue will confess that he is Lord.

For we must all appear before the judgment seat of Christ, that each one may receive what is due him for the things done while in the body.

—(2 Corinthians 5:10)

It is written:

> *"As surely as I live, says the Lord*
> *every knee will bow before me;*
> *every tongue will confess to God."*

—(Romans 14:10)

You have a choice to make. You can ask Jesus to save you and then one day live with Him in heaven forever, or reject Him and be cast into hell for eternity. Don't wait for tomorrow to make that decision because tomorrow may never come. You could die tonight and never get a chance at eternal life in paradise again. You have an important decision to make and only you can make it. No one else can help you with this. You can make reservations now to attend the big celebration in heaven one day with Jesus and his angels and your saved loved one, but it's up to you to do so. With these thoughts, I now leave you to make your decision about eternity, and I hope and pray that your decision is a wise one.

Final Words

As you have read this book, I hope that you gained a good perspective on what is going on between science, politics, and Christianity both here in the United States and all over the world. I have tried to cover the most important subjects affecting the Christian world today and have tried to briefly cover each topic according to what the Bible has to say about the subject. I did not go into extensive detail into any of these subjects. Each one could be a book of its own. My goal was to inspire enthusiasm in the mind of the reader and to encourage you to do the research for yourself.

I have spent some time trying to think of a few final words to end my work with. I have thought about many different subjects to use, but I decided to state my personal opinion on the Terri Schiavo case. This was the most unjust and saddest action I have ever witnessed in a free society. The American judicial system has failed to act with dignity and honor in a case that was truly worth investigating. Indeed these judges and others like them on the Supreme Court have absolutely too much power and authority and not enough reverence for a higher authority. In the future we must make sure that our leaders not only select honorable and trustworthy judges, but also hold these judges accountable for their actions.

Terri Schiavo was a disabled woman who was starved to death for personal gains. We all saw how the judges and the liberal mainstream news media hid the facts from the public. Once again, talk radio and the internet was my source of all information in this case. I am still not believing that this actually happened in the United States.

This country is rapidly becoming a God-hating and anti-God society forced by radical extremists and backed by even more radical judges on the Supreme Court. If we as Christians don't stand up for what is right and stand up for our personal religious freedom, liberty, and duty to the creator of life, we may soon find ourselves in a situation where it would be breaking the law to do so. It is up to all of us to select Godly leaders who will stand up for the beliefs that this nation was founded on and our constitution that was inspired by the laws of God. With this, I leave you to make your own decisions about religion, life, truth, and freedom in a country that is truly blessed by the hand of God.

What can I do?

As you have read this book, you might have wondered what you can do to get involved in America's ongoing struggle of worldly minded individuals and groups constantly attacking Christianity and the sound, moral, and ethical principles our country was founded on. You can do something. I was inspired by a single event and decided to write a book to tell others about such things. I am surely not telling you to write a book, but there are several things you can do to join the fight for religious freedom and liberty. The first thing you can do is pray. This is the most important, followed by research, or simply reading about current events involving the church that you would not normally hear on the news. The other thing you can do is vote. This is a delicate privilege in America. We have the freedom to choose our leaders and the direction of our country. I do not and will not personally endorse any specific individual candidate or political party to vote for, but there are good Christian men and women out there that do look to God through prayer for answers to the country's problems and pray for guidance in making important decisions. Voting is simple and a privilege that you should hold dear because some countries are not free to choose their own leaders. Another thing that you can do is get involved not only in your local church, but in a Christian organization with goals to preserve traditional biblical values that have been such a rich heritage in America. On the following pages I have listed organizations that might interest you. You may choose to support these organizations or join them in the fight for Christian principles for yourself, your family, and most of all for the sake and future well-being of America.

These organizations are committed to spreading the gospel throughout the world.

Southern Baptist Convention
www.sbc.org

Billy Graham Evangelistic Association
www.billygraham.org

International Mission Board
www.imb.org

www.christianity.com

www.crosswalk.com

These are organizations devoted to activating and energizing Christians to confront controversial issues. Most of these have email updates that you can sign up for.

American Family Association
www.afa.net

Focus on the Family
www.family.org

Center for Reclaiming America
www.reclaimamerica.org

Right March
www.rightmarch.com

Traditional Values Coalition
www.traditionalvalues.org

Christian Coalition of America
www.cc.org

Repent America
www.repentamerica.com

Exodus International
www.exodus-international.org

Faith 2 Action
www.faith2action.org

American Vision
www.americanvision.org

Family Research Council
www.frc.org

These are organizations or websites that are devoted entirely to the pro-life stance and the truth about abortion.

www.miraclesalwayshappen.com

www.pregancycenters.org

www.lifesite.net

American Life League
www.all.org

National Right To Life
www.nrlc.org

These are Christian and/or conservative radio shows, some dealing with Christian social issues and others dealing with national news.

American Family Radio
www.afr.net

In the Fight
www.inthefight.com

The Rusty Humphries Show
www.talktorusty.com

The Shaun Hannity Show
www.hannity.com

Morning in America
www.bennettmornings.com

These are websites and news companies for Christians who are seeking a fairer and more balanced news source. Most of these deal with issues of concern for conservative Christians with traditional values while others are just regular news services.

Cybercast News Service
www.cnsnews.com

www.thisrepublic.net

www.greaterthings.com/news

American Daily News and Commentary
www.americandaily.com

www.maxnews.com

www.bettybowers.com

www.churchcentral.com

www.truthseekersusa.net

Christian Science Monitor
www.csmonitor.com

www.freerepublic.com

www.humaneventsonline.com

www.townhall.com

The following are just a few organizations that I wanted to single out among the ones I have listed and just give a little more information about them.

The Gideons International

The Gideons are a non-profit professional men's' organization devoted to distributing bibles all over the world. It has member in 179 countries around the world who place more than 59,000,000 copies of the Bible worldwide every year for the sole purpose of winning others to Jesus Christ.

Gideons International
P.O. Box 140800
Nashville, TN 37214-0800
www.gideons.org

Alliance Defense Fund

The Alliance Defense Fund is a Christian legal organization completely devoted to defending religious freedom, the sanctity of human life, and moral values that sustain our families. Alliance Defense Fund has a legal team that works to preserve our religious freedom and heritage.

Alliance Defense Fund
15333 North Pima Road
Suite 165
Scottsdale, AZ 85260
www.alliancedefensefund.org

Liberty Counsel

Liberty Counsel is a litigation organization that is non-profit. They are dedicated to advancing and preserving religious freedom, human life, and traditional family values. Liberty Counsel is active in the courtroom against those who try to remove God from the public and challenge our religious heritage. Their win ratio is 83 percent.

Liberty Counsel
P.O. Box 540774
Orlando, FL 32854
www.lc.org

National Right to Life

National Right to Life was formed in 1973 in response to the outcome of Roe v. Wade. It has chapters in all 50 states and is devoted to spreading the truth about abortion and its consequences and also deals with other human life issues such as human cloning.

National Right To Life
512 10th Street, NW
Washington, D.C 20004
www.nrlc.org

Answers in Genesis

Answers in Genesis is a Christian organization whose goal is to advance the idea of creation by God as it is portrayed in the Bible and disproving the theory of evolution. They are currently constructing a Creation Museum that will show exhibits based on the creation of the Bible which will be a must see for all Christians who want to teach their children about God's creation. The museum will be built in Petersburg, Kentucky and is scheduled to open in the spring of 2007.

Answers In Genesis
P.O. Box 540
Hebron, KY 41048
www.answersingenesis.org

I know that there are literally thousands of Christian related organizations and groups out there besides the ones that I have listed. I have chosen the most popular and most active in society. I hope that you may take a look at each one of these groups I have listed and be encouraged, inspired, and become energetic enough to join one in order help preserve our national and personal religious freedom, heritage, and culture. Most of these mentioned have free daily email updates concerning what is going on in America and around the world and I personally have found that they are highly reliable as a news source concerning widespread lawsuits and persecution of Christians that the mainstream media refuses to report on. With these thoughts I leave you and challenge you to get active and defend your rights and freedom.

978-0-595-35667-6
0-595-35667-2

www.ingramcontent.com/pod-product-compliance
Lightning Source LLC
Chambersburg PA
CBHW020359290526
45785CB00005B/2366